Choose Me!

A play by Geraldine McCaughrean
Illustrated by Sholto Walker

In a pet shop in another dimension, the children are sitting in a row, waiting for dogs to come and buy them.

Shopkeeper: Breakfast time! I've got cornflakes for you. Here you are!

Jack: Me first!

Rory: Me first!

Mungo: Me first!

Goldy: Me first!

Terrie: Hungry, hungry, hungry!

Shopkeeper: Eat up quickly! It's time to open the shop.

The shopkeeper goes to unlock the door.

Rory: Is anybody coming? Can you see?

Goldy: How do I look?

Jack: Too keen. We all look too keen.

Mungo: It's terrible just waiting!

Terrie: Nobody's coming!

Rory: I want an owner!

Goldy: I want one!

Jack: I want one!

Mungo: I want one!

Terrie: Want one! Want one! Want one! Want one! Want one!

Shopkeeper: Calm down, everyone.

Terrie: Why? Do they like calm? I can do calm. Look at me! I'm calm.

Jack: Get washed. They like clean and tidy.

Goldy: I washed. I'm clean! Look how my shoes shine!

Jack: Don't be timid.

Mungo: Don't they like timid?

Jack: No. They like it if you rush up and say hello.

Rory: Hello, hello, hello, hello, hello!

Jack: And smile.

Shopkeeper: Don't worry. I'm sure someone will come along soon.

Goldy: What if nobody comes?

Terrie: What if nobody wants us?

Shopkeeper: Impossible.

Mungo: What if nobody wants me?

Jack: That **is** possible.

Picky Dog comes in.

Shopkeeper: Welcome! As you can see, I have many fine owners for you to choose from.

Picky Dog: Too big. No. Too small. No. Too hairy. No.

Terrie: Hello, hello, hello, hello, hello!

Shopkeeper: Oh, that's a shame. Thank you for looking, though.

Mungo: He's gone.

Goldy: I don't mind.

Rory: Nor me.

Jack: Nor me.

Terrie: Nor me. He was much too picky.

Soft Dog enters.

Mungo: She likes me better!

Terrie: She wanted me first! You stole my owner, you hairy thing!

Soft Dog: Goodness! Those two are fighting. I hate fighting. I don't want a rough person. What if I choose someone and then I find out they're rough? Can I bring them back?

Shopkeeper: No. I'm sorry.

Soft Dog: Hmmm. I'll think about it. Goodbye.

Soft Dog leaves.

Jack: She liked all of us.

Terrie: But she didn't choose any of us.

Fit Dog enters.

Shopkeeper: Welcome! What kind of owner are you looking for?

Fit Dog: I want a fit one. I'm very fit, me.
Can this one run?
Can this one jump?
Does that one swim?
Has this one won any prizes?
Which one can throw best?

Shopkeeper: Umm ... I'm not sure.

Rory: I feel tired just looking at him.

Fit Dog: Boys are fitter than girls, of course. I only want a boy.

Goldy: What a cheek!

Fit Dog: Look at them. What a feeble bunch! No good at all.

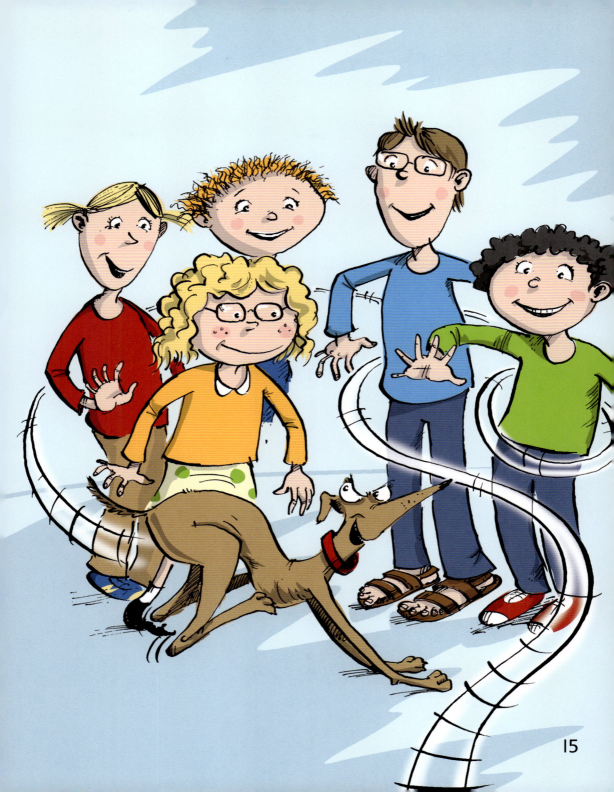

He leaves. Fierce Dog enters.

Shopkeeper: Come in! As you see, we have many fine owners here.

Fierce Dog: Well? What are you looking at, you horrible lot? Who's going to be the lucky one? You have to treat me well, okay?

These are the rules:

1. Four meals a day.

2. A collar with studs.

3. Never clean my teeth.

4. I get to sit on the sofa, right?

5. No vets, right? Never.

6. No postmen.

7. No visitors to the house.

8. And I sleep on your bed.

9. I bite, I do. Understand?

Fierce Dog: What a lame lot! I hate children. Except for breakfast. And even then they taste horrible. I'm off!

Mungo: Has he gone?

Goldy: Is it safe to come out yet?

Terrie: I was so scared!

Rory: Can I open my eyes now?

Mungo: I wanted someone to play with.

Rory: I wanted someone to love me.

Terrie: I wanted a best friend.

Goldy: I wanted someone to stroke.

Jack: I wanted someone to wag her tail when she saw me!

Shopkeeper: Someone perfect will come along – you just have to be patient.

Pooch enters.

Pooch: Hello. I'm Pooch. I'm looking for a boy. Or a girl. I don't mind.

Pooch: I promise I'd look after him or her and take them for walks every day.

I'd stand guard all night to keep away bad dreams.

I'd never poop in the house, or bite the postman. Honest!

I'd never pop balloons or join in football. Not unless I was asked.

And I promise not to jump up at the table, or put muddy paw prints on the bed or howl when the TV's on.

And I will be brave on firework night. Really I will! Quite brave, anyway. I hope.

Do you think you might have a person – one little person – for a dog like me?